Sneakers
Meet Your Feet

Sneakers
Meet Your Feet

How the World Works

by Vicki Cobb
illustrated by Theo Cobb

Little, Brown and Company
Boston   Toronto

First Edition

Library of Congress Cataloging in Publication Data
Cobb, Vicki.
    Sneakers meet your feet.

(How the world works series)
Summary: Follows the familiar materials of rubber,
cotton, nylon, and leather through the steps of
manufacturing and marketing them as sneakers.
    1. Sneakers—Juvenile literature. [1. Sneakers.
2. Shoes] I. Cobb, Theo, ill. II. Title. III. Series.
TS1017.C63 1985   685'.31   85-6895
ISBN 0-316-14896-2 (lib. bdg.)

BP

*Published simultaneously in Canada
by Little, Brown & Company (Canada) Limited*

Printed in the United States of America

10 9 8 7 6 5 4 3 2

This series is dedicated to Louis Sarlin.
the teacher who gave me the best year of my childhood
and the key to my place in the world.

Contents

The author gratefully acknowledges the help of the following people: Karen Widegren, Ken Graham, and Fred Shporer of New Balance Athletic Shoes USA, David Cohen and Pete Fanny of Fermon Leather Co., Vincent J. Cosco, Jr., of Biltrite Footwear Products, and sports podiatrist Dr. Howard Liebeskind.

Sneakers
Meet Your Feet

1.
News about Shoes

Remember the day your sneakers were brand new? Maybe you wore them out of the store. Every step you took felt different. You could tell you had new shoes without even looking at them. And they looked so terrific! They had no scuff marks yet. They had their own shape. It would take a while before they began to take on the shape of your feet. On that first outing, you really gave them a workout. You ran and jumped and hopped and skipped. Pretty soon they stopped feeling strange. Your new sneakers were now truly yours.

If you're like most kids, you got to pick out your sneakers yourself. You were told which sneakers were too expensive and which did not come in your size. But there were still plenty of styles to choose from. Maybe you chose a running shoe. Maybe you chose a leather tennis shoe. Maybe you got a special shoe for playing soccer or baseball.

When your parents were young, sneakers were all pretty much the same. They were simple shoes made of canvas with rubber soles. Your parents prob-ably didn't wear sneakers every day. But modern sneakers are not as simple. They may have more than 20 different parts. They are lightweight yet strong. They are built to protect your feet when you are most active. They do their job well. And they're fun to wear. Lots of kids wear them all the time.

Long ago shoes were made by hand. A good shoemaker made one pair of shoes a day. Shoes were

very expensive. One pair of shoes was worn for years and years. Shoes were passed on from one kid to another as they outgrew them. Today shoes are made in factories. Shoemaking is broken down into steps. There's a different person to do each job to make a sneaker. It took more than 20 people at the sneaker factory to put your sneakers together. Suppose your sneakers are made of leather and nylon fabric and rubber. Each material was made in other factories.

There are factories that just make shoelaces, for example. More than 100 people played a part in making your sneakers. They each did their job. They were paid to do it.

The money you spend for new sneakers goes toward paying all the people who helped make them. True, the money from one pair of sneakers is not much. But in the United States more than 113 million pairs of sneakers a year are bought for kids under fourteen. That kind of money for a product is called a "market." If you buy sneakers you are part of this market. All the people who help produce sneakers for the sneaker market are called an "industry." And industry could not exist without a market.

An industry and a market make the world work. Money from the sneaker market pays the people who make sneakers. Everyone gets what they need. You get sneakers and workers earn money so they can buy the things they need.

There's a story behind your new sneakers. This story starts with your feet and what they do. Then it's a story about rubber, the amazing stuff that's used for soles. It's a story about the manufacturing of leather and cloth. It's the story of the sneaker industry, of buying and selling so that many people can earn a living. It's the story of how many different sneaker manufacturers try to get you to buy their shoes, not someone else's. Different sneaker manufacturers compete for your money.

As a sneaker buyer, you are part of the world that supports the sneaker industry. You help decide which manufacturer will make the most money in the marketplace. In a small way, you are part of what makes the world work.

Discover how the world works to bring you sneakers. Read on!

2.
Meet Your Feet

Want to hear about two amazing natural wonders? You happen to be very attached to them. Meet your feet. These two small platforms each support half of your body weight when you are standing still. No other animal stands quite like we do. Most divide their standing body weight among four feet. Every step you take adds to the load on each foot. If you weigh 60 pounds, there's 120 pounds of pressure on each foot for *every* step when you walk. Running punishes them even more. When you run, each foot pounds the ground with a force of up to 300 pounds. In a soccer game of 10,000 running steps the pounding adds up. Your feet take a beating of 3 million pounds!

They can take it. Every day your feet walk or run between five and ten miles. They take you more than 70,000 miles in your lifetime. That's as if you walked two and a half times around the earth. Walking and running are not the only moves your feet can do. They can jump and skip. They can kick a football or stop short on a basketball court. Ballerinas can dance on the points of their toes. Your feet are built to walk barefoot on grass. But mostly we walk on hard surfaces. So we need shoes to protect our amazing feet.

What if we didn't wear shoes? Some people in the world don't. Usually they have a different way of life. Often they live in jungles or forests or grasslands where it's warm. The bottoms of their feet become very tough. The skin gets very thick. Such thick skin is called a *callus*. Calluses form wherever the foot rubs

against a surface. Your foot can protect itself. If your foot rubs against your shoe, first you get a blister, then you get a callus. If you went barefoot all the time, the bottoms of your feet would make their own kind of leather.

Your feet are built to take a pounding. There are 26 small bones in each foot. When you take a step, your foot flattens and your bones spread apart. When you lift up your foot, the bones move together again.

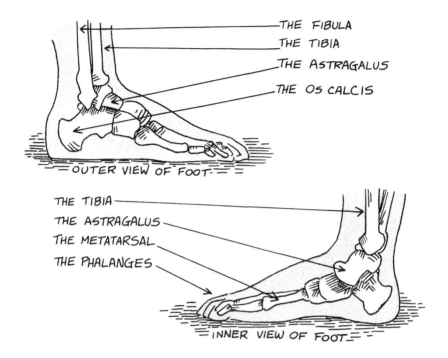

THE FIBULA
THE TIBIA
THE ASTRAGALUS
THE OS CALCIS

OUTER VIEW OF FOOT

THE TIBIA
THE ASTRAGALUS
THE METATARSAL
THE PHALANGES

INNER VIEW OF FOOT

Your feet are like springs that absorb the force of each step. Look at the bottom of your foot. The arch is where the spring is. People who are flatfooted have no springiness to their feet. Every step pounds their whole foot. The pounding goes up the leg bones. Flatfooted people often have tired feet and legs.

Ever notice the feet of apes and monkeys? They are our closest animal relatives. Their feet are more like hands. They can grab things with their feet. They use both their feet and hands for walking. Our feet are not used for grabbing things. The thumb is now a great toe. The job of the great toe is to push us forward with each step. It no longer has the job of picking things up. But the great toe can still act like a thumb.

See for yourself. Take off the shoe and sock of your favorite foot. If you are right-handed, you will also be right-footed. Hold out your favorite hand palm

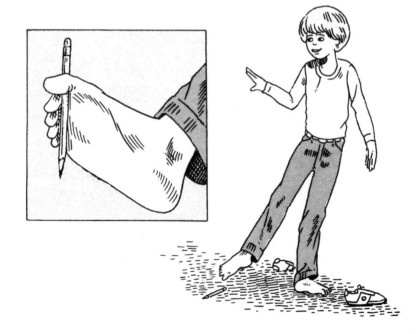

down. Move your thumb in and out. Now try and make the same motion with your great toe. You may have to think about what you're doing. But if you practice you can do it. Your toe can make the same moves as your thumb. Can you pick up a pencil with your toes? People who have lost the use of their hands learn to use their feet to do the same jobs.

Your feet change as you grow. When you were a baby you had flat feet. Arches appeared when you were about four. The most important thing you can do for your feet is to make sure your shoes fit properly. You should not have to break in shoes for comfort. They should feel comfortable right from the start. Always leave about an inch between your great toe and the tip of the shoe. Your shoes should be wide enough to allow your feet to spread when you step down. Grown-ups have foot problems mostly from wearing shoes that don't fit correctly. You don't have to make the same mistake.

3.
Rubber

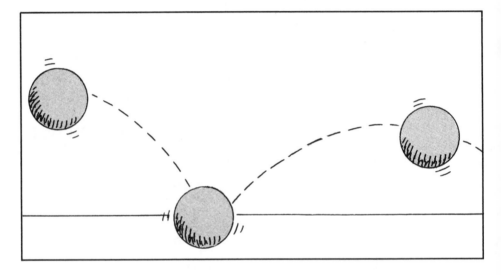

Sneakers are called "sneakers" because you can sneak in them. "Sneak" means you can walk so that no one hears you coming. Why can you sneak in sneakers? Because the soles are made of a soft, bouncy material known as rubber.

Indians from the West Indies and South America were the first to discover rubber. They made cuts in the trunks of certain trees in their jungles. A sticky white sap oozed out of the cuts. When the sap was wet it could be shaped or spread on surfaces. When it dried it turned to light brown. It now bounced. The Indians made rubber balls out of it and made up ball games. It was also waterproof. They dipped their feet in bowls of the stuff. When it hardened they could walk more comfortably in swampy areas. Their rubber "shoes" protected them from bites from swamp insects.

You can see what this natural rubber is like. Paint some rubber cement on a china dish. When it is dry rub the film you painted. You can roll it up into a ball. It is light brown. If you drop your little rubber ball on a hard surface, it will bounce.

Of course, the Indians didn't call this stuff "rubber." They had their own name for it. Rubber got its name after Europeans discovered the New World and brought some back home. An English scientist found that this dried, bouncy sap could rub out pencil marks. So he called it "rubber." You can erase pencil marks with your little dried-cement ball. And you can use rubber bands and the soles of your sneakers as erasers. Don't take my word for it. Try erasing and see for yourself.

Inventors were excited by the discovery of rubber. They felt that rubber was good for more than bouncing balls and erasers. But there was a problem with this rubber. If the weather got hot, it became soft and sticky. If the weather was cold, it was stiff and could crack. Then, about 150 years ago a man named Charles Goodyear solved the problem. He mixed rubber with a yellow mineral called *sulfur*. Then he heated the sulfur-rubber mixture. When the rubber cooled it

was firm and dry. It stayed that way when the weather was both hot and cold. It still had its bounce. Rubber that has been heated with sulfur is called *cured* or *vulcanized* rubber. Vulcanized rubber could be used for shoes.

Most of the rubber used for sneakers doesn't come from rubber trees. Scientists discovered how to make rubber from petroleum. Some man-made rubber is just about the same as natural rubber. Rubber that has not been heated with sulfur is called *raw* or *uncured* rubber. Uncured rubber can be natural or man-made. Both natural and man-made rubbers must be cured to be useful.

The rubber soles on the bottom of your sneakers are not made by the sneaker factory. There are factories that just make rubber soles. They buy raw rubber from rubber factories and turn them into rubber soles. Then they sell the soles to the shoe factory. Here's how they do it.

Making the bottoms of your sneakers is something like making cookies. First you have to mix the "dough." There are different ingredients that go into making the kind of rubber you need for sneaker soles. A basketball sneaker will be used on a wooden gym floor. Its sole is different from that of a running shoe or a tennis shoe. So the first step is to measure the different rubbers and chemicals that make the kind of sole you want. All of the ingredients are solid. So you need a really powerful "mix master" to mix them together. The rubber-sole factory has one. It's called a Banbury mixer. A giant screw in the Banbury can mix 500 pounds of ingredients into a huge, smooth blob.

The next step is to roll out the rubber, just as you would roll out cookie dough. Instead of a rolling pin, the rubber-sole factory has rolling mills. Huge rollers smooth out the blob into a sheet that is the right thickness for soles.

Next the rubber sheet is cut in the shape of a sole. Believe it or not, these shapes are called *biscuits*. The biscuits are placed in metal molds. The molds have the exact shape of the sneaker sole. They also have the pattern of the ridges and studs for the bottom design.

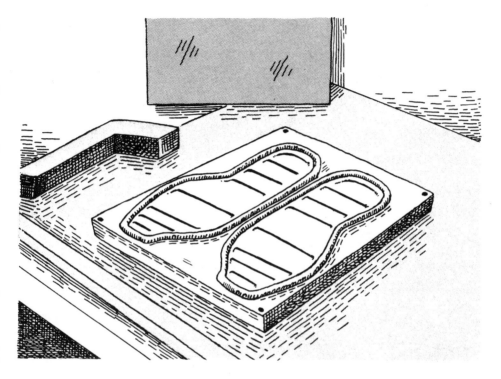

The biscuits in the molds are now baked in an oven. The biscuits melt and fill the molds. The heat cures the rubber. When the molds come out of the oven, the rubber soles are ready to become part of your sneakers.

Molded rubber becomes the bottoms of your shoes. They are called the *outsoles*. Outsoles have two important jobs. First, they grip the surface and keep you from slipping. Second, they wear well. They can take the rubbing and pounding of your steps longer than other materials. Just above the outsole is a lightweight cushion called a *midsole*. Midsoles are made of another material that can act as a shock absorber. This material can't be used as an outsole because it won't wear as well. But it does make your steps feel bouncier. Inside your sneaker is still another manufactured sole called an *insole*. It is made partly from soft, spongy foam rubber. In your sneakers you may be walking on as many as 9 layers!

The sneaker manufacturer calls the different materials and the parts of sneakers *findings*. Findings are bought from suppliers. Suppliers turn rubber into findings for the bottoms of your sneakers. Another group of suppliers provides the findings for the tops of your sneakers, called *uppers*. That's what the next chapter is about.

4.
Cloth

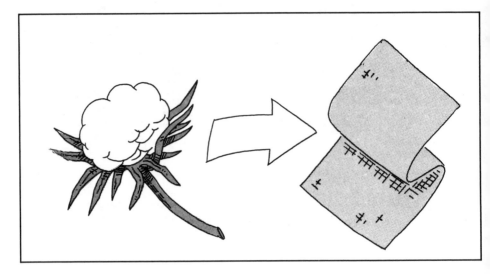

Sneakers were invented more than 100 years ago. The first sneakers were called "tennis shoes." They had rubber soles and white canvas uppers. The white canvas matched the long white pants worn by tennis players. For many years canvas was the only kind of material used for uppers.

Canvas is cloth woven from heavy cotton threads.

Cotton comes from cotton plants. Cotton plants are grown on farms in warm parts of the world. White flowers appear about three months after the seeds are planted. The flower petals change color from white to dark yellow, then to pink and finally to dark red. The petals fall three days after the flower blooms. A green pod is now where the flower was. It is called a *cotton boll*. The boll continues to grow. It turns brown. It is shaped like a tiny punching bag. The boll dries out. Finally it splits open. Fluffy white cotton bursts out.

The ripe cotton boll is made of millions of very thin threads called *fibers*. A bunch of fibers is attached

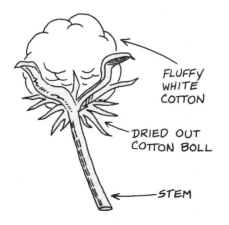

FLUFFY WHITE COTTON

DRIED OUT COTTON BOLL

STEM

to each seed in the boll. There are about 15 seeds in each boll. It is the job of cotton fibers to act like parachutes for the seeds. The wind can then carry the seeds to some other place where they can fall to the ground and sprout. Dandelions are other flowers you may know that have fiber parachutes. But most of the cotton bolls are picked long before they have a chance to be blown apart by the wind. Instead, the cotton fibers will be used for making cloth.

The cotton bolls used to be picked by hand. But today machines do the most of the work of picking cotton and turning it into cloth. The first stop for the picked cotton is the *cotton gin*. The cotton gin cleans the cotton bolls. It removes dirt and leaves. Then small circular saws pull the seeds out of the fibers. The cleaned cotton is pressed into large bundles called *bales*.

The cotton bales go next to the *textile mill*. At the mill, the fibers are cleaned again and fluffed up. Then they are combed. This combing lines up all the fibers in the same direction. If you pull on combed cotton fibers, they stick together. You can draw pulled

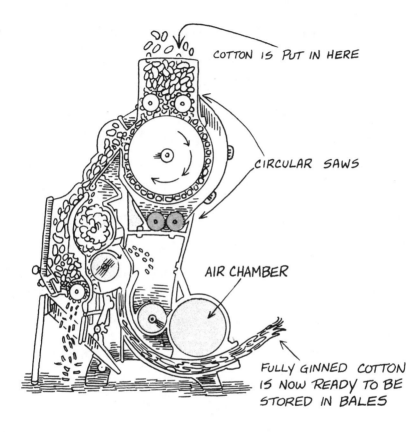

COTTON IS PUT IN HERE

CIRCULAR SAWS

AIR CHAMBER

FULLY GINNED COTTON
IS NOW READY TO BE
STORED IN BALES

fibers out. If you twist the drawn-out fibers, you can make a thread.

See for yourself. Get some cotton from your medicine chest. Pinch some and pull it away from the rest. Twist the pulled-out fibers. You can get a very short thread where you twist the cotton. Pull on your thread. More fibers will be pulled out. Twist these drawn-out fibers. Your thread will get longer.

Years ago people pulled on combed cotton fibers by hand and twisted them into thread. The machine they used was a *spinning wheel.* Every few minutes they had to give the wheel a push to keep it spinning. Some spinning wheels were kept moving by a foot pedal. It might take several days to spin enough thread to make a yard of cloth. Today miles and miles of thread are spun every minute by powerful spinning machines. Electricity runs these machines. The threads become cloth when they are woven or knitted.

The machine that weaves cloth is called a *loom.* First hundreds of threads are strung next to each other along the length of the loom. They are all going in the same direction. These threads are called the *warp.* Then new threads are added one at a time across the warp. Each new thread goes under and over warp threads. You can see a simple under-and-over weave on a tennis racket, where the strings are far apart. In cloth, the threads are close together. It takes lots of

cross threads to fill the warp. But modern looms can weave 450 filler threads a minute and turn out 100 yards of cloth in an hour. That's enough cloth to stretch the length of a football field!

Canvas is woven from heavier cotton thread than other kinds of cotton cloth. Thick canvas can take a lot of wear and tear. Some uppers of sneakers are still made only of canvas. So mills that make canvas are suppliers for sneaker factories. They ship rolls of canvas cloth to sneaker factories, where they will become uppers.

Canvas is not the only cloth used for the uppers of sneakers. Many sneakers are made partly of nylon. Nylon fibers do not come from a plant. They are man-made from chemicals that come from petroleum. Nylon fibers are made by forcing melted nylon chemicals through tiny holes. When you squeeze toothpaste out of the tube you can see how a nylon fiber is formed. But instead of coming out of one opening, nylon is squeezed out of many tiny openings like a shower head in your bathroom. Instead of getting one big fat shape, lots of thin fibers form as the melted nylon hits the air. Nylon fibers can be twisted together to make nylon thread.

Nylon threads can be woven into cloth for sneakers. But knitted nylon is used in sneakers as well. Your sneakers may have both knitted and woven nylon.

Knitting machines make cloth from one or two very long threads. Knitting is a way of making tiny loops in the thread that lock into other loops. It's easy to tell the difference between woven cloth and knitted cloth. You can see the under-and-over threads in a weave. You can see the loops in a knit. Check the ragbag in your house. An old sheet is woven cloth. If there is a torn edge, you can pull threads away. A fringe of threads remains behind. An old T-shirt is knitted. Knit stretches more easily than woven cloth. You can see loops if it is torn.

Nylon is strong and dries very quickly. It wears well. It is shinier and smoother than canvas. But it is not as thick. So nylon that will be used for sneakers is made thicker by becoming one side of a "sandwich." The nylon that will be on the outside of the shoe is stuck to a layer of foam rubber. This gives it thickness. But foam rubber can be rubbed thin if it is directly against your foot. So a thin layer of knitted

WEAVE

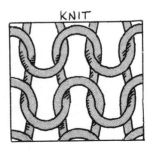

KNIT

nylon is stuck to the other side of the foam rubber. This knitted nylon becomes the lining on the inside of your sneaker. Such layered material is called a *bonded fabric*. The tongue of your sneaker is a good place to see if your upper is made of bonded fabric.

Bonded nylon fabric arrives at the sneaker factory in huge rolls. It comes in many colors. Rolls of canvas arrive at the sneaker factory. They are mostly white. But they also may come in different colors. Spools of thread that match the cloth come from another supplier. Laces of all colors come from the laces factory. The person who orders the findings has an important job at the sneaker factory. He or she makes sure that the factory has everything needed to make each style of sneaker. Production can't begin until all the findings are at hand.

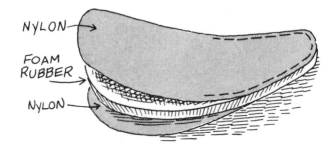

5.
Leather

Leather is a third kind of material used for uppers. Sometimes an upper is all leather. Sometimes it is part leather and part cloth. Leather that is used for uppers has also come a long way from where it started.

Leather comes from the same animals that give us beef. It is made from the skins, or "hides," of cattle.

The hides are cut off the cattle in one piece. This happens at the factory that cuts meat and packs it for supermarkets. The fresh hides are put in salt water and shipped to a factory, called a *tannery*, that makes leather.

At the tannery, the hides are put in huge drums with some very strong chemicals. These chemicals remove all the hair from the hides. They stay in the drum for three days. The drum turns, making sure that the hides are always mixed with the chemicals. It smells like rotten eggs around the drum. When a hide is removed, it is white and hairless. But it is still soft like meat.

Next the hides are put into other huge wooden drums. Different chemicals are put in the drums. These chemicals contain minerals. The minerals can enter the hides and preserve them so that they won't rot. The process of preserving animal hides is called *tanning*. When a hide comes out of this drum it is stiff like leather. But tanning has not made it tan. It is now blue.

The freshly tanned, blue hides are piled up on wooden trays. They are wet and very heavy. The pile of hides is wrapped in plastic to keep from drying out. The heavy piles are moved from one place to another in the tannery by small forklift trucks. The tanned hides are not ready to be used for shoes. Now the tanned hides must be made into the kind of leather the sneaker manufacturer wants.

The tanned leather is too thick to be used for sneakers. And the thickness is not even. Some places are thicker than others. So the wet hides go through a machine that splits them to the right thickness. Then they go through a machine that shaves them and makes them an even thickness. Workers feed the wet hides into the splitting machine and the shaving machine. Then they pile up the hides into bundles.

The hides are next put into large drums like the ones they were tanned in. But now they will be dyed. Sneaker manufacturers want leather in colors that go with the cloth. So the blue hides go into the dyeing drums and come out white or red or green. The sneaker

makers choose the colors they want when they order the leather. If they want pink leather, they can have it!

After the leather is dyed, it is dried. A worker pastes the skins onto a huge metal plate. The plate moves the skins into a tunnel of hot air. The plate moves slowly. After three and a half hours the skins come out of the other end of the tunnel. They are pulled off the plate. They are dry but stiff.

Next the skins are put through mills that roll them until they are soft. A lot of the leather that will be used for sneakers is brushed. Brushing give the leather a surface that is like velvet. Leather that feels like velvet is called *suede* (pronounced "swayed"). Leather with a smooth surface is also used for sneakers. Some sneakers have both suede and smooth leather on them. Do yours?

The finished leather is trimmed to remove parts that aren't perfect. Then each piece is measured. This way the leather manufacturer knows just how much is shipped. And finally, the soft, thin, colored leather is shipped to the sneaker factory. Soon it will be on some kid's feet.

6.
The Sneaker Factory

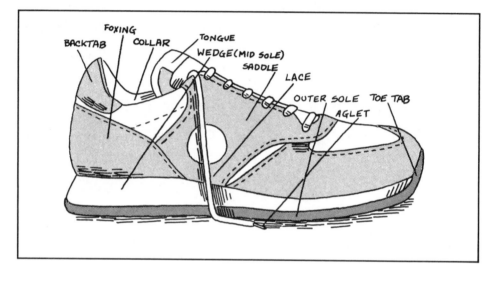

You've probably eaten homemade bread. You may own a sweater your grandmother knitted for you. But have you ever heard of homemade sneakers? They don't exist. Sneaker making is not a hobby. Sneakers are made in sneaker factories. People buy sneakers made in factories for the same reason that they buy cars made in factories. Sneakers are not simple to make. Here's why.

Sneakers are made of many different materials. Pieces of these materials have to be put together so that they stay together. No one wants a shoe that falls apart with wear and tear. Heavy-duty sewing machines are needed to stitch the uppers. Special machines are needed to attach uppers to soles.

Materials that become sneaker parts are flat. Leather, canvas, and nylon are flat. Rubber is manufactured in flat sheets. But your foot is not flat. It has lots of different curves. It is thicker in some places than others. Somehow the flat materials have to be put together so that they fit around an object that has a very odd shape.

It would take a long time to make a pair of sneakers by hand. A pair of handmade sneakers would be very expensive. Most people would not want to spend so much money. A factory can make many pairs of sneakers in one day. The manufacturer makes money by selling lots of sneakers. So he doesn't need to charge so much for each pair.

Sneaker making has been broken down into many steps. There is a different worker for each step. All the workers are called an *assembly line*. The flat ma-

38

terials are handled at the beginning of the assembly line. Finished sneakers come out at the end of the line. An assembly line of 50 people can produce 300 pairs of sneakers a day. Here's how they do it.

Cutters cut out all the pieces. They don't use scissors. Instead, they use shapes with sharp metal edges called *dies*. A die is like a cookie cutter. A strong press comes down on a die and stamps out a piece of leather or cloth. By using dies, cutters make sure that each piece is exactly the right shape.

Next all the pieces for uppers go to the sewing room. Each worker does a different stitching job. As the pieces move from one worker to the next, the

① CUTTERS CUT OUT ALL THE PIECES USING DIES.

② ALL THE PIECES FOR THE UPPERS GO TO BE STITCHED TOGETHER

uppers are stitched together. After the uppers are finished they are ready to become a sneaker.

The secret of the shape of a shoe is an object called a *last*. A last is a plastic form in the shape of a foot. The upper is joined to the sole around a last. The last makes sure that a sneaker has the shape of a foot.

First the upper is attached to the last. Then the insole and midsole are cemented in place. Finally the bottom sole is cemented on. A heavy press makes sure that there is a strong bond holding the sole to the upper.

After the bottoms are cemented on, they are trimmed. Any extra sole is removed. The sneakers are cleaned of extra cement. Finally the lasts are pulled out. Shoelaces are put in. The shoes are inspected.

The inspector makes sure that the bottoms are flat and that both shoes are the same size. They are packed in boxes and stored in a large building called a *warehouse*. Here the boxes of shoes are loaded into trucks. They have been sold to a shoe store. Truck drivers will make the delivery to the shoe store where you can buy them.

7.
Pick a Pair to Meet Your Feet

Each sneaker manufacturer wants you to buy his sneakers. So he hires people to try and figure out how to get you to choose his shoes. It's their job to make smart guesses about the things you think about when you are in a shoe store. They decide what kind of sneakers to make for you. If they guess right, you are more likely to buy their sneakers.

The price of the shoes must seem right to you. If you think a pair of sneakers is too expensive, you won't buy them. On the other hand, the manufacturers want to make money. They want to sell sneakers for more than it costs to make them. This extra money is called a *profit*. The price you pay for sneakers includes the profit. Naturally, the manufacturers want as big a profit as possible. Their problem is to find a way to make a profit while keeping the price low enough so you'll buy their sneakers.

One way to solve this problem is to keep the cost of making sneakers as low as possible. You can see how they do this. Look for a label inside your sneaker. Maybe it's on the inside of the tongue. Maybe it's printed on the side. The label will tell you where the sneaker was made. It might say "Made in Taiwan" or "Made in Korea." These are countries in the Orient. It is cheaper to live there than in America. Oriental workers get paid less than American workers. It is cheaper to make shoes in the Orient than it is to make shoes in the United States. So children's sneakers are all made in the Orient and shipped to the United States.

Sometimes you may buy a pair of sneakers on sale. The store has decided to lower the price and make less profit. It's important for them to sell the shoes they have on hand. This way they make room for new shoes coming in.

Your new shoes must fit. There should be one inch between the tip of your great toe and the front of the shoe. This leaves room for growth. Modern sneakers don't have to be broken in. They should feel comfortable when you walk in them in the store. Don't choose shoes that pinch or squeeze. New sneakers should not give you blisters.

You choose shoes for the kinds of sports you play. A running shoe is different from a tennis shoe or a baseball shoe.

You choose a style you like. Here's where it's hard for the sneaker makers to make smart guesses. Maybe you'll pick the same shoe as your best friend. Maybe you'll pick sneakers that a famous athlete wears. Maybe

RUNNING SHOE

TENNIS SHOE

BASEBALL SHOE

you'll pick sneakers that go with your favorite outfit. Maybe you won't know why you like one pair better than the others. You just do. How can they know what you'll like?

They can only guess. They give you a choice of many different styles and colors. They hope there is at least one pair to please you. And they put ads in newspapers and magazines to tell you about their sneakers. You are more likely to pick a pair that you've heard about.

Suppose there was only one company in the world that made sneakers. If you wanted sneakers you would have to buy theirs. They would not have to give you a choice in style. They could make the price as high as they wanted. You either paid the price or had no sneakers. This sneaker maker would be a *monopoly*.

It is against the law to be a monopoly. In our country, anyone can try to make sneakers for the sneaker market. It is called a *free market*. The sneaker companies in a free market compete for your sale. A company that charges too much will lose. A company that makes sneakers that fall apart will lose.

When you choose the sneakers that meet your feet, you help keep the market free. You will always have a choice. Yea!

Index